Juicy Whims

Oh, the whims of juice, so rich and bold,
Each drop a story, sweet tales unfold.
A splash of fun, a giggle or two,
With every sip, laughter comes through.

Limes and oranges, a vibrant crew,
Joining forces, what mischief they do!
Slipping and sliding, they bounce with glee,
In this juicy whimsy, come laugh with me!

A grapefruit grin, a berry surprise,
With citrus tricks that tingle our eyes.
So take a dive in this fruity spree,
Where every chuckle is wild and free.

In every bowl, a flavor chase,
With laughter sparkles all over the place.
Juicy whims make hearts ignite,
As we giggle bright under the moonlight.

Colorful Affection

In a world of colors, we frolic and play,
With citrus hues brightening the day.
Each fruit is a friend, a friend that delivers,
With kindred spirits, we're giggle givers.

Fruits of the rainbow, let's paint our glee,
With juicy affections just you and me.
Bananas blush, while berries grin,
In the sweetest moments, we dive right in.

A tangerine smile, a pomegranate twist,
By fruity delight, who could resist?
So gather those colors and dance around,
In this colorful hug, joy can be found.

We'll toast with laughter, unleash our cheer,
In fruity affection, there's nothing to fear.
Colorful dreams, a jubilant call,
With every fruity kiss, we'll conquer all!

Love's Refreshing Quench

A cool embrace in summer's glow,
Sipping sweetness, feeling flow.
All my worries melt away,
Like frosty drinks on sunny days.

A splash of joy in every sip,
Life's a ride, we take a trip.
Lemon laughs and limey dreams,
Life tastes better, or so it seems.

Laughing Citrus

In a bowl of treasures, they all reside,
With zesty smiles, they come alive.
Peeling laughter, bright and bold,
Their juicy jokes, never old.

Squeezed in morning, a citrus cheer,
Bouncing off walls, it's all we hear.
Tart little giggles, sweetened delight,
A funny fruit dance, oh, what a sight!

The Sun's Golden Fruit

Golden spheres in the midday sun,
Chasing shadows, oh what fun!
Their laughter echoes, zest in the air,
Sour and sweet, a playful affair.

Rolling down hills, they take a ride,
Bouncing around, no need to hide.
Witty banter in every slice,
It's citrus comedy, oh, so nice!

Hints of Happiness

Whispers of joy in every bite,
Sipping sunshine feels just right.
Bubbles of laughter, light as air,
Smirks and grins, with zest to share.

Tangled in laughter, a citrus gig,
Chasing frowns, they do a jig.
In fruit-filled bowls, joy takes its place,
A burst of happiness in every face.

Echoes of Citrus Gardens

In gardens blooming with vibrant cheer,
Citrus chuckles fill the sphere.
Slicked up with humor, light and spry,
Let's squeeze the fun, oh me, oh my!

With each little squirt, a giggle's unleashed,
Juicy tales of laughter, never ceased.
Fuelt by sunbeams, they come alive,
Citrus comedy helps us thrive!

A Flavorful Farewell

In the kitchen, a dance of zest,
Citrus fruit puts taste buds to the test.
Lemon laughs as it rolls away,
While orange giggles in sunny display.

Pineapple grins, never alone,
Tropics bring joy, like a joyful tone.
But grapefruit smirks with a bittersweet flair,
Says, "Don't forget, I'm still here to share!"

Citrus Embrace

When life gives you lemons, make a sweet pie,
But grapefruit chuckles, "Oh, give it a try!"
With a wink and a peel, it brings a grin,
Sour or sweet, where to begin?

In a bowl, they all meet, a fruity brigade,
Tartness and sweetness, a grand parade.
Grapefruit giggles, takes center stage,
"A citrus embrace? It's all the rage!"

Fragrant Whispers of Dawn

Morning light spills, with scents so divine,
Grapefruit whispers, "Oh, I'm simply fine!"
With a splash of sunshine, the day comes alive,
A fruity chorus, where flavors thrive.

Banana and kiwi join in the fun,
Telling tales of sweet dreams, one by one.
But grapefruit chimes in, slightly absurd,
"Let's peel back layers, let joy be heard!"

Sunset in a Slice

As dusk settles slow, colors ignite,
Grapefruit slices gleam, a beautiful sight.
A sunset so sweet, yet a twist of the tart,
Fruit friends gather, each playing a part.

The apple sings low, the berry joins in,
But grapefruit declares, "Let the party begin!"
With laughter and juice, they raise a toast,
To flavors and friends, we love the most!

The Sweetness Between Us

Juicy laughter fills the air,
As we share a zesty stare.
Peeling layers, one by one,
Sweet surprise, oh what fun!

Wedges bright, like playful dreams,
Sour notes and sugar beams.
Each bite bursts with laughter's tease,
Life's a dance, oh can't you see?

Sun-kissed Connections

Beneath the sun, we sit and munch,
A ripe delight with every crunch.
Split in two, yet whole, we cheer,
Our giggles soft, a citrus sphere.

Warmed by rays, we plot and play,
Zesty puns throughout the day.
With every slice, we toast anew,
Sweet sunshine shared between us two.

Bitter-Sweet Longing

A tangy twist of fate appears,
With pouts that hold both laughs and tears.
Soured love can make us grin,
A bitter truth we both dive in.

Taste of longing on the tongue,
With every word, our hearts are strung.
Fleeting moments, ripe with mirth,
The dance of flavors, love and worth.

The Tasting of Time

Sipping joy as clocks go round,
Each moment's flavor, newly found.
Racing tongues through seasons bright,
Savoring bites of pure delight.

Time slips by like citrus zest,
A tangy whirl, life's crazy quest.
From sweet to sour, blend and swirl,
In every taste, our laughter twirls.

Citrus Horizons

Sunshine in a bowl, what a sight,
Zesty smiles that shine so bright.
Peeling laughter, pith and zest,
In citrus realms, we find the best.

Sour faces turn to glee,
Squeezed jokes flow, just wait and see!
Juicy puns that burst and pop,
In this fruity fun, we'll never stop.

A fruit parade with vibrant cheer,
Flavorful friends gather near.
Orbiting joy in each ripe bite,
Citrus dreams take joyful flight.

Lemonade laughter in every squeeze,
Witty whims float on the breeze.
With tart rejoicing, we toast our day,
In citrus antics, we laugh and play.

A Zesty Affection

Tropical giggles in every slice,
A tangy dance, oh so nice.
Juicy jokes drip down like rain,
In sweetest segments, we find our gain.

Puns like juice; they drip and splash,
Zesty quirks that make us laugh.
Keen on flavors, both bold and bright,
In this playful world, we light up the night.

Twists and turns with every peel,
Each embrace of zest, oh so real.
Sour hearts turn sweet, you see,
In this comedy of fruit, we're free!

A citrus serenade, so divine,
With giggles spritzed, we intertwine.
Lively like a fruit-filled jest,
In this tangy love, we're truly blessed.

The Aroma of Joy

Fragrant fun wafts through the air,
With citrus vibes, we shed our care.
Twisting fragrances meet the nose,
A joyful blast, the laughter flows.

Squirrels dance on sunlit grass,
As bowls of joy begin to amass.
We squeeze the day with laughter's might,
In zesty moments, hearts take flight.

Lime-green giggles, orange delight,
Citrus frolics keep spirits bright.
With every slice, a chuckle grows,
In this citrus world, anything goes!

Bubbling joy in every sip,
With tangy stories, we take a trip.
In vibrant flavors, we discover bliss,
A whiff of laughter, oh, what a twist!

Unearthed Pleasures

In a bowl of sunshine, gleefully bright,
A split in the fruit, oh what a sight!
A burst of laughter, juice flies wide,
Sweet tangy moments, can't let this slide!

With every wedge, giggles abound,
Sipping the drips, what fun we found!
Poking the pulp, a sticky delight,
We slurp and we squirt, oh what a fright!

Orange Blossoms in the Air

Sweet scent dances, a fruity tease,
Whispers of zest ride on the breeze.
A peck on the cheek, oh so divine,
Just don't get sticky from that ripe line!

Laughter erupts from juicy bites,
Nibbles and gags, such silly sights.
Two friends with fruit, making a mess,
Painting the day in citric finesse!

Echoes of Summer

As the sun beams down, laughter rings,
Unlocking joys that summer brings.
Witty quips with every slice,
Juicy giggles, oh, how nice!

In the shade, we munch and play,
Punchy tastes brighten our day.
Sticky fingers, they leave a trace,
Memories made with a tangy embrace!

Juicy Rendezvous

We rendezvous for a citrus fling,
Tasting the joy that summer can bring.
With each right peel a giggle is found,
Sipping the sunshine, till all is drowned!

Who knew fruit could be this wild?
Zesty moments that leave us riled.
A combination of wit and zest,
A fruity feast, oh what a jest!

The Flavor of Longing

In a garden of citrus, where dreams do sprout,
A fruit with a flavor that brings us about.
It winks with a zest, oh so daringly bright,
A tart little secret that dances in light.

With each juicy bite, my heart does a flip,
Is it love or just hunger? A juicy romance trip.
I ponder the sweetness, the tang, and the cheer,
While wearing a grin as I devour my fear.

The sun on my cheek, it whispers so bold,
The nectar of joy that never gets old.
It jests with my taste buds, a laugh in the air,
A citrus encounter, I can hardly bear.

When shadows do creep, and sorrow may roam,
I summon this flavor, it feels like home.
A giggle, a twirl, a fabulous scene,
The sweet fruit of longing, oh what could have been!

Orange Dreams

In the land of bright peels, where visions take flight,
I dream of a citrus that tingles with bite.
The sun-kissed delight, it giggles and gleams,
Painting my mornings with zany, sweet dreams.

There's chaos in breakfast, a splash and a fling,
As juice flies like confetti—oh, what joy it brings!
A dance of bright flavor, a twirl and a spin,
It's yellow and orange, let the fun times begin.

In mugs full of sunshine, I sip and I sigh,
With each zesty gulp, my worries run dry.
Laughter erupts as the tang fills the room,
In a citrusy symphony, we banish our gloom.

Orange dreams tickle, they're wily and sly,
In a breakfast brigade that's so sprightly and spry.
With every last drop, I declare with a cheer,
Let's live in this moment, with zest and with beer!

Juiced Emotions

Squeezed into mornings, emotions take flight,
In a whirl of bright flavors that feel so right.
A splash of this laughter, a dash of that glee,
I'm swimming in juice; oh, what could it be?

The blender's a DJ, spinning tangy delight,
As I shimmy and shake in the morning light.
Each gulp is a giggle, a bubbly affair,
With every sweet sip, I forget all my care.

A twist of a peel, and the chaos will reign,
These juicy concoctions can drive you insane.
With friends by my side, we chuckle and cheer,
Mixing joy in a glass, while forgetting our fear.

So bring on the sweetness, let laughter ignite,
In the mix of our lives, we'll take every bite.
Let's raise a glass high, as the funoverflows,
In the world of emotions, let's see how it goes!

The Peel of Desire

A twist and a turn, oh what a delight,
The peel of the fruit keeps my heart feeling light.
With zany intentions, I chase after zest,
As laughter erupts, it's a fun-loving fest.

Colors collide, like a carnival scene,
With juicy frustrations, but never too mean.
I flirt with my breakfast, it tickles my soul,
Each wedge is a wonder, my quirky goal.

In the peel of my longing, I find such a treat,
As I dance with the flavors and skip on my feet.
A splash of bright humor, a dash of good cheer,
With the peel of desire, I'm never austere.

So let's zestfully mingle, tart laughter in tow,
With my citrusy love, I let the world know.
In the bright morning sun, where the fun shines so clear,
The peel of my heart keeps my moments so dear!

A Tender Zing

In the morning, a splash so bright,
Orange and yellow, what a sight!
A squirt on pancakes, a zingy game,
Breakfast giggles, who's to blame?

Juicy segments, out they pop,
Sipping sweetness, can't quite stop.
The laughter bubbles in every bite,
Who knew fruit could be such a delight?

Mimicking a giggle, oh what a tease,
A prank at brunch, if you please!
Pithy punchlines in every squeeze,
Fruity humor brings me to my knees.

So bring the slices, don't delay,
Let's frolic with fruit in a zesty way!
Jokes and juice on a sunny day,
With every laugh, we'll swing and sway.

Liquid Sunshine

Sipping on joy from a sunny cup,
Liquid happiness, let's drink it up!
A splash of zest with a jolly grin,
Let the chuckles and laughter begin!

Bright and tangy, it calls my name,
Not quite citrus, but oh, how it came!
Mirrors of sunbeams, glistening gold,
The taste of summer, stories untold.

Shake it up with a wink and a twist,
Each drop a giggle that can't be missed.
Sip and sway like it's a dance,
In every gulp, there lies romance!

Pour it out, make a joy-filled wave,
The toast of sunshine, bold and brave!
Each laughter shared, each silly face,
In liquid joy, we find our place.

The Tang of Togetherness

A bowl of fruit, what a silly scene,
The tangy tease, in oranges they gleam.
Slice them up, let's share a laugh,
With juicy bits, it's a fruity craft!

Juggling segments, watch them fly,
Dodge the pithy as they come by.
The more we munch, the louder we cheer,
In this citrus chaos, we shed our fear.

Squeeze of friendship in every meal,
From sunrise smiles to the evening feel.
A toast to laughter, so bright and clear,
We're squeezed together, oh, what a cheer!

So gather round, let's take a bite,
With segments of joy, it feels so right.
In tangy laughter, we'll always stay,
United in fun, come what may.

Essence of Summer Days

Waking up to a citrus beat,
Juicy flavors, can't be beat.
Sunshine in slices, ripe for the day,
A tangy laughter, come out and play!

With each twist, the giggles flow,
Slicing fruit, oh what a show!
Sharing bites, a fruity cheer,
Summer's essence, let's persevere!

Splashes of color, a picnic delight,
Lemonade dreams, take flight in the light.
Whisk away worries with a zesty cheer,
In this fruity folly, we've nothing to fear.

So raise your glasses, toast to the sun,
With tangy sweetness, we all have fun.
Let's soak in laughter, in this warm play,
The essence of summer, come seize the day!

Sweet Summer Sorrows

In the sun we dance, so bright and bold,
With laughter loud, and stories told.
A splash of juice, a twist of fate,
The citrus fate, we can't await.

Lemonade dreams and orange peels,
Squeezed too tight, oh, how it feels!
But sweet tang can make us grin,
With every bite, let the fun begin!

A summer patch of tangy fun,
Under the sun, all woes are done.
A citrus slice, a wild delight,
We giggle away into the night.

So raise a toast, to this fine day,
With fruity whispers, come what may.
For every drop of joy we find,
Summer sorrows can be so blind.

Citrus Lullaby

Close your eyes, hear the fruit's sweet song,
In a world of zest where we belong.
With every squeeze, a giggle spills,
The fruity dreams bring hearty thrills.

Peaches blush and lemons laugh,
In this orchard's humorous half.
Tartness dances, sweetness sings,
While chuckling birds play silly flings.

Grapes and limes in merry cheer,
Join the fray and draw us near.
A nighttime tale of bright delight,
Where citrus dreams dance in moonlight.

So hush your doubts, let worries fade,
In fruity realms, we'll parade.
Through tangy worlds, we twirl and sway,
In this lullaby, we laugh and play.

Original title:
The Grapefruit's Kiss

Copyright © 2025 Creative Arts Management OÜ
All rights reserved.

Author: Clara Whitfield
ISBN HARDBACK: 978-1-80586-349-6
ISBN PAPERBACK: 978-1-80586-821-7

A Burst of Sunshine

In the morning light, so bright,
A citrus grin brings delight.
Laughter bubbles, sweet and clear,
Like juice that splashes, full of cheer.

Peeled and pitted, oh what fun,
Each slice sparkles, just like sun.
Wedges dance, a tangy jig,
Who knew fruit could make you gig!

Zestful Heartbeats

A zingy beat within my chest,
With every bite, I feel so blessed.
Citrus whispers in my ear,
A cheerful tune that draws me near.

Juicy dribbles, what a mess,
Wearing orange? Yes, I guess!
Puckered smiles and silly grins,
In this love, we both win.

Citrus-Tinged Memories

Sun-kissed days and silly nights,
Citrus laughter, pure delights.
Skimming peels with playful flair,
Memory bursts, a fruity rare.

Glee is found in tiny bites,
As flavor dances, heart ignites.
Every splash, a splash of fun,
Twist and turn till day is done.

Orchard's Caress

In the orchard where fruits play,
A citrus dance brightens the day.
With a wink and a silly grin,
Let's roll and munch until we spin.

Dressed in peels, we twist and shout,
Squeezing joy, there's never a doubt.
A zesty giggle, a fruity tease,
Oh, how these flavors aim to please!

Sunshine beams from every tree,
Bouncing laughter, wild and free.
Sipping juice, we make a mess,
Still we sing, no time to stress!

Under branches, the wild party,
Each bite's a laugh, a zestful hearty.
With every squeeze, a smile's near,
Join the fun, bring on the cheer!

Sunlit Rind

Golden rays on juicy scenes,
Squeeze the day, forget the beans.
Wobbly fun in citrus bliss,
Who knew that fruit could bring such a hiss?

With every bit, a giggle flies,
Sweet and sour, a fruity surprise.
Run through orchards, jump and sing,
This day's the best, let laughter ring!

Bouncing notes like a jolly tune,
Underneath the broad sun's boon.
Slice it up, have it your way,
With a splash of zest, brighten your day!

Sipping nectar, we start to glide,
In this fruit parade, there's no need to hide.
Juicy joy, oh what a bind,
In each bright bite, life's redefined!

The Flavor of Desire

Craving laughter, a tangy zest,
A fruit-filled dream is simply the best.
Twisted peels and bright cheery hues,
Let's munch together, we just can't lose!

Sticky fingers, laughter bursts,
Sweet surprises quench our thirsts.
With juicy bites and silly schemes,
Our fruity fun fuels wild dreams.

Under sunlight, we take a chance,
With every drop, it's a fruity dance.
Savoring moments, we twist and giggle,
Joy in our hearts, we laugh and wiggle!

Beneath the branches, let's make a fuss,
The flavor of fun is quite a plus.
So bring your passions, let them fly,
In a world of fruit, we laugh and sigh!

Nectar of the Morning

Morning sun and fruity bliss,
Start the day with a citrus kiss.
Freshly squeezed, we splash around,
In our world, pure joy is found.

Rolling out of bed with zest,
A fruity feast, we're feeling blessed.
Giggles rise with each new slice,
What a treat, oh so nice!

Nectar flows, our spirits soar,
With every sip, we laugh some more.
Sweet and sour in joyful fights,
Chasing dreams in sunny lights!

So peel away your worries, dear,
In this juicy realm, there's cheer.
Let's share a laugh, a citrus fling,
Life's a party, let us sing!

Sunrise Citrus Whisper

In the morning light, so bright,
A fruit rolls over in delight.
It giggles as it bounces free,
Whispering secrets, just for me.

Peeling back layers, a riddle spins,
Sweetness beneath the tangy grins.
Juicy drips and playful squirts,
A game of hide and seek, it flirts.

Orange laughter fills the air,
With zestful tales beyond compare.
Each slice a joke, a fruity jest,
In citrus sunshine, we are blessed.

Rinds roll around like playful cats,
Joining in a dance with hats.
Beneath the sun, we share our cheer,
In the orchard, fun awaits us here.

Zestful Encounters

With each new dawn, we take a chance,
A citrus fruit joins in the dance.
Lounging on a plate of cheer,
Its bright smile chases clouds from here.

A squeeze of lime, a twist of fate,
The fruit awaits, oh what a date!
Juicy giggles and tangy laughs,
A slice of life in fruity halves.

Stop and savor, play along,
The zestful dance, a silly song.
Its peels are puns, the juice a rhyme,
Each fruity bite, a taste of time.

When citrus whispers in my ear,
I laugh and grin, it brings good cheer.
In every bite, a playful tease,
With zestful encounters, life's a breeze.

Juicy Secrets of Dawn

As daylight breaks, a secret stirs,
A juicy fruit, the morning purrs.
Its tart surprise brings playful fun,
Under the warmth of the rising sun.

Beneath the skin, a world unfolds,
Sweet and sour tales, bright and bold.
Sipping juice, I spill the tea,
On all the mischief, just you and me.

The drizzle dances on my chin,
Each bite invites a cheerful grin.
Morning laughter fills the space,
With juicy secrets at our pace.

Let's toast to moments, sweet and dear,
When juicy delights bring us near.
In the dawn, our spirits soar,
With love and laughter, who could ask for more?

Tangy Embrace

In the orchard, I find my muse,
A tangy fruit that can't refuse.
With every bite, a zesty cheer,
It's just the laugh I want to hear.

Squeezed tight in a sunny hug,
Those playful peels, a silly smug.
Citrus moments swirl around,
In this embrace, joy can be found.

Spritz of flavor, a cheeky wink,
Under the tree, we sip and think.
Its vibrant hue, a burst of fun,
In tangy love, our hearts are one.

Roll a slice, let laughter flow,
With every bite, we steal the show.
In citrus dreams, we twirl and spin,
A tangy embrace where smiles begin.

Whirlwind of Flavor

In a bowl of bright delight,
A citrus swirl takes flight.
Juicy giggles roll around,
Zesty laughter shakes the ground.

Pucker up and take a taste,
Sweet and sour, never waste.
Squirting joy with every bite,
Lunch is now a playful fight!

Bouncing flavors all in sync,
Sipping sunshine from the pink.
Dancing on the kitchen floor,
Squeezing giggles, wanting more!

Like a jester in disguise,
Citrus charm brings sweet surprise.
Fruits can make you dance and cheer,
Join the party—bring good cheer!

Vivid Vows

Promising a taste so bright,
Lemonades seem dull in light.
A zestful pledge with fruity flair,
Triumphs made in citrus air.

Sassy sips and daring drips,
Cheeky smiles from juicy lips.
Brightened dreams of tangy fun,
Sour souls just want to run!

With each burst, the laughs return,
Pinky-sworn, we shall not yearn.
Life's a splash of gleeful twists,
Join the club of fruity lists.

Every sip a silly tease,
Sprightly moments put at ease.
In this circus of delight,
Flavor reigns with all its might!

Tangy Wishes

Wishes dipped in citrus zest,
Hoping for a sunny fest.
Dreams of tang and fruity cheer,
Join the fun, the taste is near!

Pineapple dances, lemons laugh,
In this silly fruit staff.
Wishing wells of sour glee,
Drink it up and share with me!

Bubbling wishes in a glass,
Fizzing joy—come raise a class.
Wondering what's next to try,
Hop aboard and drink up high!

As the tangy tales unfold,
All our wishes will be bold.
Sip and sing and laugh away,
Every day's a fruity play!

Featherlight Touch

A feathered brush of citrus glow,
Whispers sweetly, oh so slow.
Tickling taste buds, soft and spry,
Lemon puffs make giggles fly.

Gentle nibbles, teasing spritz,
Fruity flutters; don't you flinch!
A light caress that makes hearts sing,
Twirling flavors tack the spring!

Floating scents of laughter bloom,
Sugared vibes fill every room.
Softest flavor, cheeky tease,
Dancing tongues with utmost ease!

A citrus cloud on playful days,
With every sip, the heart obeys.
Here we join, a merry bunch,
In a world of zest, we munch!

Juicy Echoes of Passion

In the morning light we meet,
With citrus smiles and laughter sweet.
We share a slice and grinning wide,
A playful dance, our joy can't hide.

Splashes of zest, we can't contain,
Our silly games, like sugar rain.
With every taste, our giggles blend,
A citrus crush we can't defend.

A tangy twist, a cheeky pout,
Who knew this fruit could bring about?
The quirks of life in every bite,
Our silly moments take to flight.

So here's to us, the zesty pair,
In every wedge, a spark to share.
We'll savor joy, let laughter flow,
For in this fruit, our hearts aglow.

The Flavorful Exchange

A citrus grin upon my face,
A slice arrives, so full of grace.
Your juicy charm, my taste buds sing,
In this playful fruit, I find my fling.

Each segment bright, a giggle shared,
A dance of flavors, I am prepared.
We swap our bites, oh what a feast,
From this bright fruit, our laughter's released.

Sweet and sour, a love affair,
In every wedge, we show we care.
With sticky hands and sticky minds,
The fruity fun is what we find.

In this exchange, we taste the sun,
Dancing together, two of a fun.
So let's toast to zest, to life so grand,
In every slice, together we stand.

Tasting the Twilight

As twilight falls, the day unwinds,
With citrus hues and playful finds.
I think of you, my silly muse,
With every taste, I just can't lose.

The flavors burst, a sunlit tease,
I giggle at your next big sneeze.
Our laughter's bright, a sweet delight,
Together we shine, an epic night.

So let's indulge in tangy fun,
With every slice, we come undone.
As twilight glows, we share a wink,
The juice of life, it makes us think.

With playful banter and zestful cheer,
Each session's unique, my dear, my dear.
In every sip, our spirits soar,
This fruity life, we can't ignore.

Sun-Kissed Secrets

In sun-kissed realms where laughter dwells,
We trade our secrets, fruity spells.
With tangy giggles, we take a bite,
A juicy world, pure delight.

What's hidden within the wrinkled skin?
A playful bond that won't wear thin.
We share our whims with every zest,
These silly moments are the best.

With every slice, a secret shared,
In playful games, we're fully prepared.
A tangy spark ignites the scene,
In bustling laughter, we reign supreme.

So here's to us in citrus cheer,
We dance through life, oh so sincere.
With every taste, a joy that's fixed,
In sun-kissed warmth, our hearts are mixed.

A Dance with Sunshine

In a garden bright and fair,
Fruits twirl, spinning in the air,
With laughter echoing so sweet,
Dancing shadows on our feet.

Juicy swirls and zesty vibes,
Tiny ants in quirky tribes,
Wobbling fruits that miss their beat,
A carnival of smiles we greet.

Sunshine spills, a neon splash,
Citrus giggles, what a clash!
Tickled taste buds, what a scene,
Life's a dance, so bright and clean.

So grab a slice, come join the cheer,
With fruity friends, let's not show fear,
Together we'll all take a whirl,
In sunshine's glow, our hearts will twirl.

Dappled Light on Fruitful Hearts

Underneath the lofty trees,
Fruits grin, swaying in the breeze,
In the dappled light, they gleam,
A fruity world, a zesty dream.

Chubby cheeks with joyful glee,
Sipping juice beneath the lea,
Lemons laugh as limes roll by,
While oranges flirt, oh my oh my!

Don't be shy, just take a bite,
Zesty giggles feel just right,
With every squirt, a smile grows,
In this patch where laughter flows.

So join the fun, don't miss the show,
Fruitful hearts put on a glow,
Let's dance and snack, it's time to play,
Under the sun, we shout hooray!

Aroma of Radiance

In the kitchen, scents arise,
A citrus breeze makes dreams devise,
Whisking laughter in the air,
Peeling rinds takes us anywhere.

Zest and humor, a fruity blend,
Creating joy, our hearts will mend,
A splash of juice, a cheerful cheer,
With every squeeze, we draw near.

Sticky fingers, oh what fun,
Citrus battles, one by one,
Pulp flying, siblings yell,
In this kitchen, all is well.

So let the fragrance fill the room,
As we dance and chase the gloom,
With every bite, the world feels right,
In our heart, we'll shine so bright.

Heartstrings and Citrus Dreams

Oh, the fruit that hugs the day,
With heartstrings that pull us to play,
Kisses from zest, the laughter bounces,
Joyful hearts, oh how it flounces!

In the orchard, we find our groove,
Let's squish and twist, let's make a move,
With every squirt, the giggles spill,
Citrus magic gives us a thrill.

Whirls of colors, a fruit parade,
Sunshine dripping, never a fade,
We're singing songs of sweet delight,
In this world, everything feels right.

So gather 'round, it's time for fun,
In citrus dreams, we are all one,
With each bright fruit, our spirits soar,
In heartstrings and laughter, we'll explore.

Ripened Yearnings

In the morning sun, I spy,
A fruity treasure, oh my!
Round and plump, it waits for me,
A burst of joy, will it be free?

I take a nibble, oh what zest!
In this moment, I am blessed.
A splash of tang on my tongue,
Laughter echoes, we're just begun.

Juicy dribbles down my chin,
Like a cheeky grin, it's a win!
A citrus smile, so absurd,
Life is silly, haven't you heard?

At brunch today, I'm in a whirl,
With grapefruit slices, watch them twirl!
Citrus jokes fly, laughter's twist,
Who knew fruit could be this kind of bliss?

Aromatic Allure

In the kitchen, scents ignite,
Tangy whispers, pure delight.
Slicing through the juicy skin,
A burst of laughter from within.

Fragrant notes dance in the air,
A citrus charm beyond compare.
My friends gather, eyes ablaze,
For fruity fun in sunny rays.

With every bite, a giggle grows,
As sticky fingers steal the show.
Oh, this zest, it makes us sing,
Like silly birds on vibrant wing.

The sun dips low, the joy persists,
As we trade our grapefruit twists.
Aromatic smiles, laughter's song,
In this fruity game, we all belong.

Citrus Secrets

Underneath the morning glow,
A citrus riddle starts to flow.
What's the deal with all this juice?
It's a puzzle, what's the use?

Peelings twist in playful glee,
A tangy prank, just wait and see!
Each slice reveals a story grand,
Of fruity mischief, oh so planned.

Pink and yellow, colors bright,
A zestful dance, a pure delight.
With each laugh, a secret slips,
As grapefruit juice drips from our lips.

At the end of this grand feast,
We'll toast to fun, our joy increased.
Secrets shared in sticky bliss,
Who knew fruit could taste like this?

Vibrant Encounters

In the market, colors pop,
With every slice, I just can't stop.
A vibrant thrill, a merry chase,
Finding fruit in every place.

One bright orb caught my eye,
As laughter bubbled, oh so sly.
I offered one to a friend near,
We both munched with goofy cheer.

Juicy bites, a bumbling show,
A citrus dance, delightful glow.
With every squirt, we take a chance,
In this silly fruit-filled dance.

At sunset's edge, we'll laugh and play,
In juicy moments, we'll find our way.
Vibrant encounters, a tasty blend,
With grapefruit giggles that never end.

Citrus Serenade

In a bowl of bright delight,
A yellow globe sits tight.
With zestful grin, it laughs aloud,
Winking at the morning crowd.

Its tangy charm can't be contained,
A citrus tune, humor unchained.
Beneath the sun, it twirls and spins,
Ready to start where the fun begins.

Dancing on the kitchen floor,
With citrus giggles, we want more.
A squeeze of joy in every bite,
Life's a party, feeling just right.

So grab a spoon, let's dive right in,
Let's see who laughs and who will win.
With every segment and every slice,
This fruity jest is oh so nice!

Squeeze of Affection

A bright orb of cheerful cheer,
With pulpy hugs and love so near.
I twist and turn, can't get enough,
This playful fruit sure knows its stuff.

With every squirt, a splash of glee,
It tickles my tastebuds, fancy-free.
Juicy jokes and playful puns,
A cheeky fruit that loves to run.

Unpeeling layers, what a sight,
A zesty waltz both day and night.
In a world of lemons, it's my prize,
With heckles and giggles that never die!

So squeeze me tight, don't let me go,
This citrus love, a radiant show.
With every slice, let's make a toast,
To the funny fruit we love the most!

Morning's Fruity Flirtation

A morning sun shines bold and bright,
In the kitchen, what a sight!
A flirty slice, with nectar sweet,
Debating if it's green or neat.

With witty puns, it takes a chance,
Inviting all to join the dance.
A squeeze of sunshine, laughter loud,
While giggles gather, we feel proud.

Bouncing lightly, full of cheer,
It whispers softly, "Come near, dear!"
A citrus pal, that's quite the tease,
Bringing playful warmth with the breeze.

So let's sip juice in playful style,
With fruity smiles that stretch a mile.
In every drop, affection blooms,
Morning's kiss in cheerful rooms!

The Sweetness in Bitterness

A vibrant fruit with sassy flair,
Balances life with humorous care.
Sweet and tart, a funny blend,
With every bite, a giggle to send.

In the bowl where colors play,
It rolls around in a zesty way.
Bringing laughter to the table,
Oh, what fun! Let's not disable.

The tangy twist draws folks around,
Where every grin is truly found.
With pithy jests, it steals the show,
Mixing laughs with juice, in flow.

So here's to the zest that lifts our days,
In its bittersweet, hilarious ways.
A squeeze of dreams and laughter long,
Celebrating all that's fruity and strong!

Sweet Zest of Memory

In morning light, a burst of cheer,
A citrus smile that lingers near.
With every bite, a giggle grows,
Who knew taste could wear such clothes?

Its tangy twist, a playful tease,
Like tiny jokes that dance with ease.
We shared a slice, the juice did spray,
And laughter shared, it made our day.

Recalling days of sunny fun,
When slicing fruit was never done.
In bowls of joy, we scooped and played,
Those citrus moments never fade.

So here's to zest, our sweet delight,
In every bite, a pure delight.
With fruity smiles, we'll reminisce,
Those juicy days we can't dismiss.

Lush Gardens of Desire

In gardens green, a fragrant quest,
Where citrus dreams can feel the best.
A twirl of laughs in every gust,
Those peels of joy are hard to trust.

With every tree, a secret pact,
Of juicy feasts, who can distract?
The bees all buzz, they find it grand,
While we sneak bites with sticky hands.

Those tangy treats, they light the way,
To sunny picnics, come what may.
In each bright wedge, a tale unfolds,
Of silly smiles and moments bold.

Our laughter circles, bright and round,
In leafy shade, we're fate unbound.
So grab a slice and join the song,
With citrus dreams, we can't go wrong.

Scarlet and Gold: A Love Story

Two halves collide, a vibrant fate,
With laughter sweet, we celebrate.
Scarlet blush and golden glow,
A playful dance, a zestful show.

The taste of love, a citrus thrill,
With every sip, it fits the bill.
We squeeze the moment, let it flow,
And let the sweetness overflow.

In sticky fingers, joy is found,
As we exchange the zest profound.
With every bite, our spirits lift,
In fruity love, we find our gift.

So here's to us, a tasty pair,
With scarlet tones, we're light as air.
In every wedge, our story spins,
A juicy tale where laughter wins.

A Citrus Bouquet in Bloom

Amidst the blooms, a fragrant jest,
A citrus bouquet, nature's best.
With every whiff, ideas sprout,
And giggles tease, there's never doubt.

With oranges bright and lemons fair,
We toss a smile, without a care.
The zest of life, in petals curled,
A citrus feast, our laughter swirled.

In playful sips from cups we raise,
We toast to friendship, sunny days.
A splash of fun, a twist of fate,
In every sip, we celebrate.

So gather 'round, our joyful crew,
With citrus charms, we'll pull on through.
For in this blend, we find our bloom,
And laughter dances, bright as noon.

Citrus Trails

In the land of sunny blooms,
Where citrus scents do loom,
Fruits wear smiles on their peels,
And laughter is what it reveals.

With each juicy, funny bite,
They dance and sway in delight,
Squirrels giggle in a race,
A tangerine in a crazy embrace.

Zesty pranks and lemonade jokes,
Citrus fruit in funny cloaks,
Lemons plumped and stealing shows,
Limes balancing on their toes.

As the sun sets with a grin,
The citrus party will begin,
With splashes and spritzers in sight,
Fruit-filled laughter, pure delight.

Freshly Pressed Affections

A squeeze of joy in every glass,
Where sweet and sour moments pass,
Oranges giggle, lemons pout,
A citrus love that's never in doubt.

Squishy pears all in a row,
Wondering what the sassy fruits know,
Margaritas with a twirl and twist,
Fruit fellows jive, none can resist.

Juicy friends on a playful spree,
Smiles abound, you wait and see,
With each slurp, a citrus cheer,
Funny zingers fill the air.

So raise your glass, let's toast to fun,
In juicy moments, we're all one,
Freshly pressed, our hearts will bloom,
In this fruity, laughing room!

The Dance of Zest

In a bowl of zesty cheer,
Fruits are dancing, bring the beer!
Lime spins, and orange glides,
With grapefruit doing funny slides.

Whispers of citrus fill the air,
Peels in sync, a fruity flair,
Bananas giggle, apples sing,
While cherries twirl in a sticky fling.

Dancing feet, they shimmy and shake,
What a mess these fruits can make!
Fruit salad in a swirling spree,
Just a bit of chaos and glee.

As the night winds down to rest,
Fruity friends still feeling blessed,
With smiles wide, they share their zest,
In every laugh, they are the best.

Morning Light

In morning light, oranges gleam,
Lemons slice through the day's dream,
Mornings filled with citrus cheer,
Wake up laughter, hold it dear.

A splash of juice, giggles burst,
Jolly fruits, maybe they're cursed!
Bananas slip on tiles so bright,
As coffee brews, they start a fight.

The sun peeks in, playful and bright,
As fruits conspire for the morning bite,
Whimsical scenes, wild and fun,
In this fruity race, we've all just begun.

So raise your cups, and toast the day,
With laughter and fun in every way,
Morning light brings joy anew,
In this fruity world, we'll chase our cue.

Citrus Bright

Citrus bright upon the vine,
Sassy spritzers, feeling fine,
With a wink and coffee swirl,
Fruits will dance, a crazy whirl.

On the table, they take their stand,
Playful laughter, spritz in hand,
Juggling fruit in sunny skies,
With bursts of zest in every surprise.

Joyful moments, loud and sweet,
Tickled toes in sunshine's heat,
Apple and peach share funny tales,
While mint makes shocks with silly wails.

So come and join this fruity spree,
A citrus world, just you and me,
Each ray of sun, a vibrant kiss,
In this merry, juicy bliss.

Scarlet Skin and Golden Heart

In a grove where shadows play,
A fruit with charm leads the way.
Its blush so bold, a cheeky tease,
Gives smiles like sunshine in the breeze.

With zestful joy it greets the day,
A whimsical dance, come what may.
It rolls and bounces, causing glee,
But watch your step; it might be free!

A tart surprise in every bite,
Brings laughter loud, it's pure delight.
With hints of sweetness, oh so spry,
This fruity prankster makes you sigh.

Amidst the laughter and the fun,
Not meant for wars, but games well won.
For under its vibrant, rosy skin,
Lies the warmth that pulls you in.

Lush Tropics at Twilight

In twilight glow where colors blend,
Flavors mingle, none can offend.
The night air tickles, spirits rise,
As juicy wonders flicker eyes.

Bouncing bowls of citrus zest,
A laugh erupts from every guest.
With every slice, a sticky grin,
A funny dance as taste begins.

Laughter bubbles, tastes collide,
The sweet and sour do not hide.
In tropic fun, we lose our cares,
With friends, we share the fruity flares.

So gather round with jovial cheer,
In lush coconuts, drinks appear.
With twilight hues that stir the night,
Our feasting fails to feel polite.

Rind of Romance

In gardens lush, love takes its stance,
One twist, one bite, a fruity romance.
Its peel so thick, yet oh so sweet,
With every nib, the heartbeat's beat.

It rolls across the picnic scene,
Scattering giggles, light and keen.
Being courted by citrus charm,
No cause for worry, just pure calm.

The laughter swells with every squeeze,
As love transpires with citrus ease.
No heartstrings tugged, just citrus fun,
Romantic fate is on the run.

With every chuckle, zest shared wide,
The rind reveals a softer side.
In fruity bliss, we play our parts,
A playful jest that warms our hearts.

Kiss of Morning Juice

At dawn's first light, a fruit parade,
The morning sip, a lively charade.
With pulpy giggles, sunny surprise,
A splash of joy that energizes.

A cheeky squirt from a citrus foe,
Wakes sleepy souls; they laugh and glow.
With juggling cups and fruity spills,
The morning game is filled with thrills.

Slicing sunshine on the board,
Each drop a laugh, the taste adored.
It dances down the tongue with glee,
This morning zest, so wild and free.

In citrus moments, friendships bloom,
As laughter echoes in the room.
With every kiss of juice, we find,
A quirky start to the day aligned.

Rind and Rapture

In the morning light, I grin wide,
A fruit so bright, it cannot hide.
Peeling away, that zestful smell,
With tangy laughs, I break the spell.

Juicy globes with an orange hue,
Bouncing around like morning dew.
Slice and share, don't be shy,
A giggle awaits every time you try.

A pithy punch, a zestful jest,
This fruit knows how to jest the best.
Wedge my heart with a citrus smile,
Oh, the joy is worth your while!

When life gets tough, don't you fret,
Just grab a slice, it's a sure bet!
With seeds that dance and juice that flows,
Come laugh with me, where sunshine glows.

Sunbeams in a Bowl

A bowl of joy upon the table,
Sunlit orbs, oh what a fable!
Bright and round, they giggle loud,
In the fruit parade, they're so proud.

Vitamin C in a playful tease,
Squeeze them tight, or eat them with ease.
Zesty bites make the best jokes,
A burst of laughter in every poke.

I'll toss with glee, a salad bright,
Sunshine smiles, a pure delight.
Drench it all with a cheeky grin,
Watch the good vibes come spilling in!

As bowls get empty and time flies past,
Memories linger, smiles will last.
So take a piece and taste the cheer,
Let's raise a toast, the fruit is here!

Slices of Life

A knife in hand, the ritual starts,
Cutting through, we share our hearts.
Pale and pink, they glisten so bright,
Every slice, a laugh ignites.

Juicy drops, a citrus shower,
Laughter blooms with every hour.
Chomping down, we trade a joke,
Each segment whispers, fun is woke!

Imagine, please, a world so grand,
Where every wedge lends a helping hand.
Sour and sweet, a perfect blend,
In this zesty space, there's no end.

So slice the day with citrus cheer,
Share the joy with everyone near.
For in this fruit, we find our groove,
Laughter, love, and all things smooth.

The Language of Citrus

In the orchard's grasp, we find our muse,
Each zestful word, a playful fuse.
Sassy skins with secrets to tell,
Their fruity gossip casts a spell.

Peel away layers, hear the squeak,
Joyful banter, vibrant and chic.
Squirting splashes, bursts of cheer,
In citrus words, we have no fear.

From tangy tales of sunny days,
To juicy laughs that amaze and daze.
In every fruit, a riddle lies,
Pithy punchlines, oh what a prize!

So speak in slices, laugh it loud,
Citrus echoes, make us proud.
Join the chorus, let's uplift,
In every bite, there's joy and gift.

Squeeze of Romance

In a bowl of citrus hue,
We danced, a fruity two!
With a squirt and a splash,
Our hearts did a rash.

A pucker turned to delight,
As we twirled left and right.
Sweet tangs in the air,
With zest everywhere!

Laughter bubbled like soda,
Our love taking a moda.
With every bite we took,
A silly, juicy hook!

So let's sip and share,
This juicy love affair.
In a world so bright and bold,
Our citrus tale unfolds.

Zesty Connection

You and I, oh what a pair,
Zesty charms are in the air!
A sprinkle of humor, oh so tart,
With every giggle, we take part.

In a twist of fate we found,
A fruity love that spins around.
Juice drips down with every laugh,
Our playful moments, quite the craft!

Peeling layers, what a sight!
In laughter's glow, we feel so light.
A tangy touch that feels just right,
As we dance into the night.

So here's to zest, the funny cheer,
A slice of joy, our favorite sphere.
In this citrus world, we spin and sway,
With a zesty connection, come what may!

Dew-kissed Dreams

Morning sun on our skin,
With dewdrops we jump in.
Tasting sweetness, what a scheme,
As we share our dreams!

Sips of laughter, oh so fresh,
A fruity hug, a zesty mesh.
Each giggle brings a shine,
In a world that feels divine.

A splash of fun in every sip,
With silky fruit on a road trip.
Carried by fun, joy on the stream,
Oh, how we chase our dew-kissed dream!

So let's seize the fruity day,
With lemon zest, we'll laugh and play.
In our funny garden scene,
We bloom in our juicy sheen!

Bright Tones of Affection

In the orchard where we roam,
Bright tones of love feel like home.
With each laugh, a burst so sweet,
Together, we can't be beat.

A little zest, a lot of fun,
Juicy moments, just begun.
With a chuckle, we take our flight,
In flavors, our hearts ignite!

Wit as sharp as citrus peel,
Through every joke, we start to feel.
A playful wink, a zesty grin,
In this dance, we always win!

So here's to us, bright and bold,
In this love that never grows old.
With tones so vivid, let's embrace,
In this juicy, funny space!

Juicy Secrets Unraveled

A citrus fruit hides secrets bright,
Beneath its skin, pure delight.
With every bite, a zesty laugh,
Sour face? Nah, just my better half.

Peeled away, the truth appears,
Sweet and tangy, no room for fears.
Juice drips down, a playful splash,
I love this fruit in a silly bash.

Though messy hands might raise a fuss,
I giggle loud, no need to rush.
Let's squeeze the day, embrace the zest,
For juicy secrets come out best!

So here's to fun in every slice,
Blend of flavors, oh so nice.
We'll dance around this citrus ball,
Together we shall have a ball!

Citrus Serenade

In the orchard, laughter flows,
What's that smell? Oh, who knows!
With every bite, a burst of cheer,
That tangy jab, oh dear, oh dear!

A romantic date with fruit divine,
The juice drips down like sweet sunshine.
I think I love this zesty treat,
Each little wedge, oh what a feat!

Watch out, friend, it's quite a prank,
A tart surprise, you might just tank.
But once you taste that citrus joy,
You'll laugh so hard, you'll shout, "Oh boy!"

So sing along in fruity glee,
Citrus songs, just you and me.
A serenade that's bright and bold,
In this orchard, laughter unfolds!

Tangy Meetings

At the market, what a sight!
Citrus colors, pure delight.
I trip on peels, give a shout,
This fruity world, what's it about?

Round the stand, I spot a friend,
Grapefruit giggles, we can't pretend.
Tasting tangy bites, we just howl,
In this mad fruit race, we'll growl!

Juice on cheeks, a sticky affair,
But each sweet laugh erases care.
Let's brunch with slices, what a feast,
In each long laugh, we're joy released.

So here's to meetings, oh so bright,
With every wedge, we add delight.
Stick together, our fruity crew,
This tangy life is made for two!

Sweet and Sour Encounters

At breakfast, what a cheeky grin,
Watch out! I'm diving in!
Sweet and sour, what a mix,
With every slice, we find new tricks.

A little bitter, but so much fun,
I grab a wedge, says, "Let's run!"
The juice dribbles, laughter roars,
It's a citrus brawl behind closed doors!

From sticky fingers to big old grins,
This fruit game's where the fun begins.
A playful bite, some messy spills,
In sweet and sour, joy fulfills.

So lift your forks, let's raise a toast,
To every citrus, here's the most.
In laughter's light, we can't resist,
These flavors wrapped in a fruity twist!

Peel Away the Shadows

In a world of zesty delight,
I found a fruit, oh what a sight!
With a twist and a pop, it's so divine,
A citrus giggle, I've lost track of time.

Underneath the skin, the laughter hides,
Juicy secrets that the mouth confides,
Each wedge a joke, a punchline spritz,
Who knew fruit could give us such fits?

The sun's shining bright, humor in tow,
As I bite into sweet citrus flow,
Pulp and pith, they're in on the jest,
A laugh-filled feast, I must confess!

So peel away all that's dire,
Let's dance with zest, fuel the fire!
In a world of laughs, we'll surely bask,
With every bite, I can't help but ask!

Sunset's Citrusy Caress

As day gives way to evening's glow,
A tangy grin begins to show.
With the sun dipping low, I take a sip,
This citrus drink, a joyful trip.

The stars above seem to wink and sway,
In laughter's chorus, they're here to stay.
Zingy notes in twilight air,
A giggle here, a chuckle there.

Each drop dances on my eager tongue,
Making a symphony, oh so young!
With every taste, I break into song,
A quirky tune that can't be wrong.

So raise a glass, let laughter ring,
In the sunset's warmth, our spirits cling.
With every sip, the fun begins,
In citrus magic, we all win!

Citrus Bloom under Moonlight

Under a moon so big and bright,
Citrus blooms whisper tales of delight.
With every petal, a chuckle so bold,
Juicy stories waiting to unfold.

The night air is filled with sweet perfume,
While fruits giggle in the quiet gloom.
With each drop of dew, the green leaves sigh,
As sneaky smiles float up to the sky.

Slice it up, and let the fun explode,
This citrus love is the perfect ode.
Zesty laughter echoes through the trees,
Dancing with joy in the gentle breeze.

So come join the party, let's all partake,
In moonlit magic, our hearts awake.
With citrus dreams and chuckles to share,
In laughter and love, we find our flair!

The Flavor of Yearning

Yearning flavors call my name,
Citrus cravings, a tasty game.
With every slice, a wish takes flight,
In bursts of laughter, we find delight.

I dream of zest, of tangy fun,
Bright juices spark when day is done.
With each sip, a giggle escapes,
As ripe dreams play with juicy grapes.

As sunset casts its golden glow,
Oh how my citrus passion grows!
In every twist, a yearning tingle,
Life's perfect punchline, making me jingle.

So here's to cravings that dance and tease,
With fruity humor that aims to please.
With every bite, let laughter flow,
In the flavor of longing, let's steal the show!

www.ingramcontent.com/pod-product-compliance
Lightning Source LLC
Chambersburg PA
CBHW060127230426
43661CB00003B/358